Lie Down
and
Roll Over

Lie Down
and
Roll Over

and 159 other ways to say I love you

BY JIM ERSKINE AND GEORGE MORAN

CLARKSON N. POTTER, INC./PUBLISHERS, NEW YORK

Distributed by Crown Publishers, Inc.

Printed in the United States of America
Published simultaneously in Canada by General Publishing
Company Limited

DESIGNED BY BETTY BINNS GRAPHICS

Library of Congress Cataloging in Publication Data

Erskine, Jim.
  Lie down and roll over.

  1. Love—Anecdotes, facetiae, satire, etc.
I. Moran, George, 1942–   II. Title.
PN6231.L6E7   1981   818'.5407   81-12085
ISBN: 0-517-545241

10   9   8   7   6   5   4   3   2   1

FIRST EDITION

Susie, this one's for you!

J. E.

They do not love that do not show it.

JOHN HEYWOOD

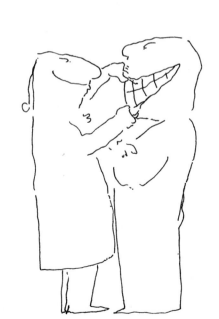

Admire his teeth.

Forgo the small talk.

Burn your little black book.

Warm his socks.

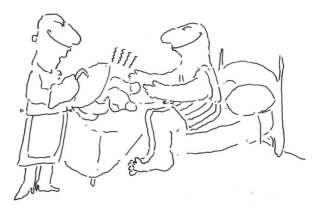

Cook him a heart-shaped meatloaf.

Swear you love her on a stack of Bibles.

Remember her birthday.

Carve your initials on a tree.

Crawl through fire.

Knit Siamese sweaters.

Dress up like Cupid.

Pull in your stomach.

Lower the blinds.

Put her on a pedestal.

Move mountains.

Run out of gas on Lover's Lane.

Build a shrine.

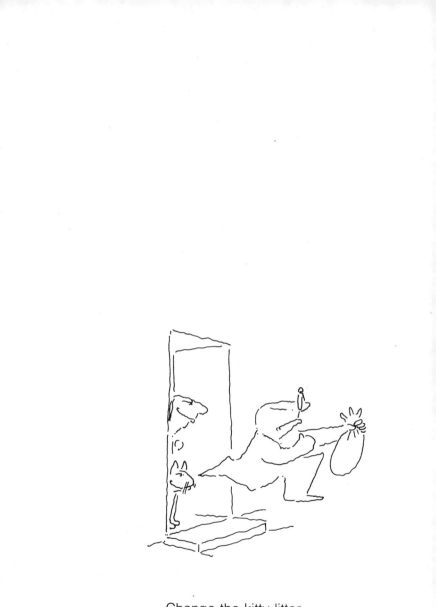

Change the kitty litter.

Be an animal.

Paint hearts on her toenails.

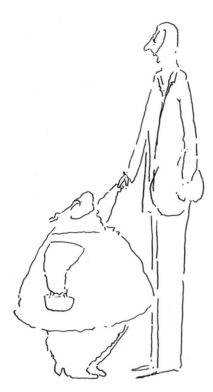

Ignore each other's faults.

Smell flowers together.

Eat all your spinach.

Lie down and roll over.

Draw little pictures for her amusement.

Hold hands.

Watch the sunrise together.

Carry a torch.

Cherish every hair on her head.

Buy a love potion.

Sacrifice yourself.

Buy her a mink.

Hand her the world on a silver platter.

Bring her a tuna on rye, no mayo.

Get all the lumps out of the mashed potatoes.

Protect her from all harm.

Bring her a nice fat juicy frog.

Swim the seven seas.

Break out the satin bedsheets.

Drop your defenses.

Hide little surprises.

Peel a grape.

Name your dog after him.

Give up your bad habits.

Listen intently.

Ask if she's lost weight.

Like all her friends.

Share your ice cream.

Put something extra in his piggy bank.

Don't do your Groucho Marx imitation.

Button up his overcoat.

Pick the lint off his clothes.

Massage her scalp.

Anticipate her every need.

Save all the red jelly beans.

Play footsie.

Dedicate a song to her on the radio.

Share all your secrets.

Make bewitching facial expressions.

Applaud when he enters the room.

Be his electric blanket.

Put the stamp on upside down.

Save him a place in line.

Flatter her mother.

Put on lots of whipped cream.

Cheer her on.

Hide a love note in his lunch box.

Shout it from the mountaintop.

Confide in strangers.

Do the dishes.

Roll out the red carpet.

Order one soda, two straws.

Dine by candlelight.

Go out and close the garage door.

Take her shopping.

Talk mushy.

Diet together.

Empty the mousetrap.

Take the blame.

Smother her with kisses.

Strike alluring poses.

Worship the ground he walks on.

Give each other a bath.

Camp on her doorstep.

Dazzle her.

Turn out the lights.

Write a sonnet.

Wear seductive aromas.

Get his and hers hairdos.

Give her a life-size replica of yourself.

Be passionate.

Forgive and forget.

Wrap yourself around her little finger.

Laugh at his jokes.

Snuggle.

Take all the seeds out of the watermelon.

Glue yourselves together.

Let him read your diary.

Make a baby.

Blow kisses across the room.

Serenade her.

Quote Shakespeare.

Give her half your baseball cards.

Mail yourself to her.

his dreams.

him on your knee.

Vary your kisses.

Strew chocolate chip cookies in his path.

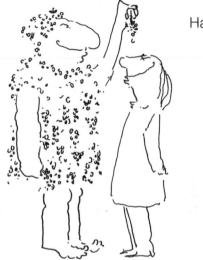

Hang mistletoe everywhere.

Invade

Bounc

Pretend you are her favorite dessert.

Paper the walls with his picture.

Tattoo her na

Bronze his s

Fly her to the moon.

Share your french fries.

Go dancing.

Carry her across puddles.

Pick up the check.

Arrange special little breakfasts.

Inspire each other.

Write his name everywhere.

Whisper sweet nothings in her ear.

Make a commitment.

Sew your initials on his underwear.

Dangle upside down in front of her.

Rub up against her leg.

Gaze into her eyes.

Rock him to sleep.

Run toward each other in slow motion.

Paint her portrait.

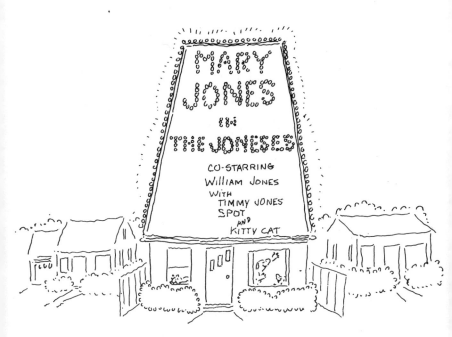

Put her name up in lights.

Get out of the kitchen.

Pre-chew his food.

Let her get into the lifeboat first.

Play peekaboo.

Put violets on her pillow.

Nibble his toe.

Serve him chicken soup when he's sick.

Tweak his cheek.

Share a chair.

Wear suggestive clothing.

Start a fan club.

Be her Tarzan.

Elope.

Bat your eyelashes.

Be gentle.

Weave garlands for his hair.

Handcuff your wrist to his.

Don't fight.

Send him a valentine every day.

Drink champagne from each other's slippers.

Hire a violinist.

Scratch his itches.

Nudge her with your nose.

Share your sleeping bag.

Follow him to the corner and wave good-bye.

Throw yourself at him.

Let her sleep.

Move in.